Empath

How to Find Your Sensitive Self and Use Your Gift to Heal and Help Others While Protecting Your Positive Energy

Natalia Adams

Table of Contents

3

Introduction

You are about to dig into a journey that will support you with understanding, uncovering and deepening your connection to yourself as an empath. In this book, you are going to discover exactly what it means to be an empath, what parts of yourself are affected by being an empath and what you can do about being an empath.

In today's world, the word "empath" is frequently used in various forms of spiritual, psychological and self-development texts that are meant to support people to further understand their sensitive side. With that being said, sometimes, the information floating around can make the term itself seem a little confusing, as there tends to be a lot of information floating around identifying what an empath is and why some people are empaths in the first place.

To help you really get an understanding of what this unique trait is, why you have it, how it can help you and what you can do to protect yourself as an empath, I have written this book just for you. I want this book to be your go-to resource when it comes to an understanding of who you are and how you can support yourself in having a better quality of life going forward. Many empaths find that they are not adequately supported in their journey and, as such, they struggle to feel seen and get the help they need when it comes to being incredibly sensitive.

Before you can begin understanding what it means to be an empath and what you can do about it, it is important for you to know exactly what this aspect of yourself is. It is also helpful for you to recognize whether or not you actually identify with this aspect of yourself so that you can understand if you truly are an empath.

According to Dr. Judith Orloff, a trained psychiatrist, an empath is someone who empathetically *feels* what other people are feeling to the point where it can be challenging to decipher one's own feelings from another person's feelings. With that being said, being empathic is different from being empathetic, as empathetic is something that can often be controlled, whereas being empathic seems to be a continuous state of being. In other words, empathic people cannot "turn off" their empathy. It is always on and always connecting them to other people and other people's emotions and experiences.

Science has shown that people who are empaths actually have differences in their brains that contribute to them being empathic. In particular, their mirror neuron system tends to be hyperactive. The mirror neuron system is the system in the brain that creates empathy by having an individual witness certain energy or emotion in another and then beginning to experience that energy and emotion within themselves. Through this change in how their mirror neuron system behaves, empaths quite literally experience intense, constant feelings of empathy for everyone around them.

Being an empath is not necessarily something that is diagnosed in people. Instead, it is more something that we identify and recognize within ourselves and that we move forward with, using a deeper sense of self-awareness and compassion towards ourselves. With that being said, there are certain things that you can do to identify whether or not you are an empath.

The easiest way to find out if you are an empath is to ask yourself the following questions:

1. Am I often told that I am "overly sensitive" or do I identify as a shy or introverted person?
2. Do I find myself feeling drained after spending time in crowds?
3. Are being overwhelmed and anxiety feelings I experience often?
4. Do I find myself getting overwhelmed by excessive noises, odors or people who talk a lot?
5. Do I have physical reactions, such as illness, from arguments or yelling?

6. Do I have any chemical or physical sensitivities?
7. Do I regularly feel like an outcast in various situations?
8. When I go out, do I generally take my own car, so I can leave early if I need to?
9. Do intimate or close relationships give me anxiety or discomfort?
10. Do I tend to have strong reactions to caffeine and medications?
11. Is my pain tolerance generally low?
12. Do I find myself gravitating towards nature for a chance to replenish my energy?
13. Do I have strong relationships and "communication" with animals and nature?
14. Do I find myself feeling better in smaller cities or in the country, versus busy cities?
15. Do I find myself needing a lot of alone time to recuperate from being around people who are difficult or who require a lot of my energy?

If you answered "yes" or identified with all or most of these questions, then chances are, you are an empath. This means that you, like other empaths, have a tendency to experience deep connections to other people and their emotions and energies, even when you do not know those people so well.

Being an empath is a great thing, but it is often depicted as a bad thing by many people who are empaths because they have not yet learned how to handle being one. When you are an empath with no strong coping mechanisms, it can feel like you are constantly at the mercy of others, which can certainly stimulate the belief that your empathic abilities are a curse more than they are a blessing. However, once you begin to understand what it means to be an empath, why you are one and how you can protect yourself and use it as a gift rather than a curse, being an empath feels a lot more enjoyable.

Generally, people who are empaths and who lack coping skills feel that they are constantly being thrown around by life. They may find themselves feeling as though there is no hope for them to engage in "normal" life because they struggle to engage with other people or do things that regular people do. Some empaths even find themselves struggling to the point where going to work takes up so much of their energy that they spend every minute after work trying to recover and rebuild their energy from the experience. This can lead to the feeling of constantly being isolated and even feeling lonely despite the fact that social isolation was a choice to attempt to minimize the stress that comes with being around other people.

When you do not know how to manage your emotions and your energy and you find yourself struggling to be around other people, it can feel like something is seriously wrong with you. Many empaths think they have a problem and will never be able to enjoy life the way other people enjoy it because there is simply no chance that they can ever "adapt" to social norms. Naturally, this can make you feel like your blessing is actually a curse and like you will always be stuck this way.

Fortunately, being an empath does not have to be like that. Once you realize that the purpose of being an empath is to help people and *that* is the reason that people are always so attracted to you and your energy, things can begin to change. With this realization, you can understand why everyone around you seems to come to you for help or crave your energy. This is because people see you as being someone they can benefit from knowing, as you will have the answers, as well as emotional and energetic support that they need to feel better about their own troubles in life. As an empath, in a way, it is your job to be there for them to help them and support their healing so that people can begin to have more positive experiences in their lives.

In the bigger picture, your purpose is to help the planet heal from the deep lack of compassion and emotional connection that everyone seems to be suffering from. Your purpose is to work together with other empaths to "wake people up" to the reality of their own suffering and trauma so that they can begin to heal themselves and experience more freedom from their once-painful realities.

Many empaths find that once they realize that this is their purpose, a lot of their previous experiences in life begin to make far more sense. Suddenly, it is easy to understand why so many people sought you out and shared their life story with you, even though you had just met them 30 seconds ago and you never even had the chance to introduce yourself. It also makes sense why everyone around you seems to be so "damaged" and why they are constantly coming to you to "fix them".

Despite the fact that helping others is your purpose, it is important to understand that, even as an empath, you are still a human. This means that you still need to focus on how you can honor your own energy and take care of yourself. Just because you have the capacity to heal and help others does not mean that it is your job to do so around the clock. In fact, there is no hard and fast way to determine *how* you are going to do this. What can be determined, however, is what feels right for you and how *you* want to go through life helping other people.

When you can begin to identify what type of helping feels good and what type of helping you are good at, you can also begin to identify strong boundaries that you can use to protect yourself. Through protecting yourself, you can stop feeling like you are at the mercy of people who are struggling to control their own emotions and healing. And then you can start feeling stronger within your own energy. This creates the opportunity for you to use your empathic gifts more intentionally and to stop feeling as though your energy is constantly being dragged all over the place by people, such as energy vampires who are inconsiderate of your energy and well-being.

If you still feel as though you identify with everything being said and you are ready to learn about how being an empath is a blessing and not a curse, then it is almost time for you to begin reading *Empath*! Now that you know that all of this resonates with you, you can feel confident that what you are going to learn within this book is going to help you step into the next level of what it means to be an empath. With that being said, I invite you to take your time with this journey, as it can be quite overwhelming for some people.

As you read through *Empath*, I invite you to take your time and read through it at your own pace. I have laid this book out in a way that will support you in building on your knowledge, but if you feel that you need certain pieces of knowledge more than others, feel free to bounce around and read the chapters that resonate most with you. The ultimate goal here is to ensure that you have all of the support, guidance and education that you need to heal your wounded empath self and begin enjoying a more intentional and purposeful existence as an empath. This way, you can enjoy your gift *and* the world around you.

Now, if you are ready to begin, let us get started!

Chapter 1: Types of Empaths

Believe it or not, not every empath is made the same way. Even though all empaths tend to have the same general differences going on in their minds in response to other people's energies and feelings, not every empath is here with the same purpose or method for using their gifts. In fact, not everyone experiences their gifts in the same way, either.

Understanding what type of empath you are and what that means is a great opportunity for you to deepen your understanding of yourself and have a greater ability to support yourself along this journey. It is important that you understand that despite how many resources exist for you, at the end of the day, exploring your empath self is a personal journey and you are the only one who can truly work with this information. That means it is up to you to identify what resonates most with you and what information you can use to help you have a more peaceful experience in your life as an empath.

With all that to be said, before we dig deeper, let us take some time to uncover what type of empath you are and what that means about your unique gift. Below, you are going to find out how you can identify what type of empath you are. And then, we will discuss all the types of empaths so that you can understand the differences between each type and how do they differ with your type.

What Type of Empath Are You?

The easiest way to find out what type of empath you are is to write down in your journal or on a piece of paper all of the ways that you experience your empathic gift. After you have done that, you can listen to the following six types of empaths and see which resonates most with who you are and what you wrote down. You might find that you resonate with various types of empathic gifts.

However, you should find that one or two types are more dominant than others. The type that you find more dominant is your "empathic type".

Emotional Empath

Emotional empaths can pick up the emotions of others around them and feel the effects of those emotions as if they were their own. Often, emotional empaths feel things incredibly deeply and may carry others' wounds as if they were their own. For example, if you see someone who is hurting or someone who told their story about a trauma that they experienced, you might begin hurting, too and you might need to heal and release from that trauma, even though it is not your own. As an emotional empath, your goal is to learn how to differentiate between your own emotions and other people's emotions so that you do not become drained from emotional interactions.

Medical Empath

Medical empaths can feel the energy of another person's body and, in some cases, may feel the pain of others in their physical body too. For example, if someone around you has a headache, you may also begin to have a headache because you can empathically feel their headache. Medical empaths often get diagnosed with autoimmune diseases, like fibromyalgia, caused by their ability to feel other people's pain. As a medical empath, your goal is to learn how to turn this empathic gift off as needed so that you are not always absorbing other people's symptoms.

Geomantic Empath

Geomantic empaths can feel the energy of a physical space or landscape in a way that can be hard to describe to others. If you find that some spaces help you feel comfortable and others make you uncomfortable or even anxious, especially for no apparent reason, you are likely a geomantic empath. As a geomantic empath, your goal is to learn how to live in harmony with your environment and your purpose is to protect it.

Plant Empath

Plant empaths have the ability to feel and intuitively communicate with plants. If you can "hear" what plants are saying to you to the point where you intuitively know what they need and how to care for them, you are likely a plant empath. Plant empaths often find that they also receive wisdom and knowledge from plants too. Your goal as a plant empath is to learn how to communicate with them even better and to advocate for the well-being of plant life everywhere. You are an advocate for the forests, so to speak.

Animal Empath

Animal empaths have a tendency to have strong connections with animals to the point where they can sense what an animal is saying or needing. Animal empaths telepathically communicate with creatures in many ways, allowing them to share "conversations" with animals. Many animal empaths go on to become veterinarians, rescuers, caregivers and advocates as a way to work together with animals. As an animal empath, your goal is to connect more with animals and your purpose is to care for them and protect them.

Intuitive Empath

As an intuitive empath, you can pick up information from people, objects and places simply by being around them. You tend to just "know" things, simply by being in the space of another. Often, you can tell if someone is lying or telling the truth simply by the intuitive energy you pick up on. As an intuitive empath, you need to work on strengthening your energy field so that your mind is not constantly being bombarded with more information from everyone around you. Your purpose is to be able to help support and care for other people and work towards healing humanity in general.

Chapter 2: Empath Benefits

Being an empath actually has a lot of benefits that can serve you in your life. Many people do not get to experience life the way that they are supposed to, which means that many people do not get to enjoy what others enjoy. Empaths often feel like they are cursed, but the truth is they are blessed. Being able to experience life as deeply as an empath can mean that you have the capacity to truly enjoy everything that this world has to offer you. Through that, you find yourself enjoying far more of the world around you than anyone else does, which means you truly know how to have a "good time".

Understanding what your benefits are and how you can use your empathic gift to reap in the rewards of your benefits can help you have a much more enjoyable life experience. Through this, you can start to really understand why your blessing truly is a blessing and how it can bless your life in ways that most people will never get to experience.

Understanding Energy and Energetic "Signals"

The first step in being able to access your blessings is understanding what energy is and what energetic "signals" you are receiving as an empath. As an empath, you experience the environment around you at face value as others do and you experience the environment on an entirely different layer. That layer is the layer of energy.

Most empaths experience energy through their extrasensory senses. This means that there is an "extension" on your human senses of sight, hearing, touch, taste and smell that allows you to receive information about the energy of your environment. In addition to these five senses, you also pick up an inner "knowingness" that seems to come to you without any alternative sense giving you that "knowingness". This is called being *claircognizant*.

By being able to pick up extra information about your environment in this way, you gain the opportunity to experience the world in a way that is far different from how the average person experiences it. You gain the opportunity to experience the world in a way that allows you to know more than virtually anyone else does about the environment around you. That in itself leads to massive benefits for you, which can be used to enhance your life and the lives of people around you.

Having the Power to Truly Know People

As an empath, you have the unique ability to truly know people and their intentions, even when they are not outright telling anyone who they are or what their intentions are. For example, you have the capacity to know if someone is lying to you or if they are withholding information about what their true intentions are. You can also tell if someone is genuine to you, which means that you know when you should and should not trust someone. Often, this comes with a "gut feeling" that is essentially your intuition speaking to you through your empathic gifts.

In addition to being able to tell if someone is lying, you can also spot manipulators, energy vampires and people who are stuck in their victim mentality easily. Being able to spot people like this means that you know when you should put up your energetic boundaries to avoid being taken advantage of by people who are not going to respect you, your energy and your well-being. This means that once you begin to read people and know how to assert yourself, you no longer have to feel as if you are at the mercy of people who do not truly care about you and your well-being.

When you are able to spot liars, manipulators and people who tend to be abusive in their energy, you give yourself the option to choose to avoid or ignore those people. As a result, you give yourself the option to protect yourself, which is something that not many people can achieve!

It is important to understand that just because you know when someone is lying or manipulating another person does not mean that you are responsible for speaking up or confronting that person. You are not obligated to become a mediator or a hero and save the day for everyone in every situation. In fact, you are not obligated to do so in any situation. Knowing does not mean that you need to become the martyr; it simply means that you have the option to respectfully disengage from that person and avoid getting wrapped up in their toxic cycles.

Clearing Your Own Energetic Patterns

When you have an intuitive connection with energy, you have the unique ability to read energy, as well as to work with it. This means that you have the capacity to actually identify and clear your own energetic patterns on a deeper level than most people can typically work on. When you can identify and heal your own energy, you give yourself the opportunity to go incredibly deep on your healing work and experience life in an even deeper and more enjoyable way.

There is a saying in society that goes: "you can't pour from an empty cup". Since being an empath is entirely about helping others, this means that it is also entirely about helping yourself. Your number one goal as an empath should always be to keep your own cup full so that you feel incredible and that helping others feels like a blessing rather than a curse.

Many things go with keeping your own cup full, including being able to spot your own patterns and consciously heal them. You can also use this pattern-spotting ability to identify when something or someone has disrupted your energy so that you can begin to heal your energetic experience. Anytime you have unhealthy patterns that may rule your mind or life, you should focus on how you can heal those patterns so that you are no longer at the mercy of them.

As you learn how to fill your own cup and keep yourself healthy and "full", you will find that life becomes far more enjoyable. You still have the capacity to feel deeply, but it no longer takes control over your life because you have taught yourself to put yourself first. As a result, you find yourself easily giving to others and partaking in your purpose on Earth without feeling drained and cursed for having this deep inner push to fulfill your purpose.

Increasing Your Creative Energies

Virtually, every empath has a naturally high creative ability because they are so deeply connected with so many energies that lead to inspiration and intuitive, creative downloads. As an empath, you too have the ability to be highly creative in many different ways. Chances are, you may even find yourself prone to constantly witnessing this creativity within yourself and constantly recognizing ways that you could be creative if you wanted to act on the inspiration you were receiving. Many empaths find that they are constantly "fighting off" feelings of creativity because so much constantly comes their way as a person and each one seems like an opportunity they could take advantage of.

If you are reading this and thinking "I am definitely not creative", it is a good idea to step outside of your comfort zone and reconsider what you believe to be creative. Empaths are good at everything —from creating with their hands to creating with their hearts, minds and mouths— so there is plenty that stands to be created by you if you desire for something to be created by you. You can create by making a piece of art, by teaching a class, by dancing or simply by creating with your heart.

One of the biggest keys to creating as an empath is to unlock your potential by dropping the illusion of perfection. As an empath, you might find yourself literally feeling the pressure to be perfect at everything you do in your life. This, naturally, is not healthy and will not support you with being able to create and enjoy your creative gifts. Understand that perfectionism was taught to us by a capitalist society filled with people who believe that we should be perfect at everything so that everything can be monetized. As an empath, you do not have to (or want to) subscribe to these doctrines. Instead, let yourself be messy, let your work be imperfect and create from your messy, imperfect heart. From there, true magical creations are invented and shared for the whole world to see and the energy in those creations and inventions change society as we know it.

Cultivating a Unique Life Filled With Purpose

Unlike other people, empaths tend to have deep purposes built into them, which they feel as though they truly cannot deny or overlook. You may find yourself recognizing that there is a specific passion or purpose that you have been attached to and worked for all your life with no clear understanding as to why or when this became your passion or purpose. This is common for empaths.

While it may sometimes seem like a curse that you constantly feel this deep internal call into action, your passion and purpose is actually an incredible blessing. It is important to understand, however, that having this passion and purpose does not mean that you are required to have some form of miserable life living at the mercy of your passion and purpose. For example, if you find that you are passionate about helping victims of abuse find help and healing, you are not required to become a doormat for them to walk all over as they pour out all of their worries and feelings onto you. You are not required to be available around the clock for them to pour their hearts out and lean on you if they need your assistance. You are allowed to say no and have healthy límits or boundaries and, in fact, you are required to if you are going to be able to truly fulfill your passion and purpose in life.

Once you learn how to have healthy boundaries around your passion and purpose, being an empath starts to feel a lot more enjoyable. Suddenly, you gain the opportunity to live a life that feels amazing and you gain the opportunity to fulfill your life's mission, which feels amazing in and of itself. Many people never get to experience what it's like to have a wildly deep life calling, as well as the pleasure of fulfilling that calling, so stepping into your empath self and embracing this part of you can be a huge and powerful benefit.

Being Bold Enough to Be Your Authentic Self

As an empath, another benefit you gain is the ability to be your authentic self. With your gift of being able to read and experience energy, you have the ability to identify who you truly are and which parts of your personality have been "adopted" from society's standards and teachings. This means that you have the unique capacity to shed the masks that society has placed on you, identifying what your true beliefs are and digging into your authentic self and authentic expression.

Being able to feel who you are and knowing your truth means that you can break out of the prison of limiting beliefs and limiting stories that you have been told and you can start living as who you truly are. This means that you can connect with the deepest parts of who you are and be your true self and live with freedom of expression. This is a blessing that many people will never get to experience.

The more you get to know who you are and the more you begin to develop boundaries around your empathic experiences, the more you will be able to express as your true self and the less you will live at the mercy of others. Through this, you will find yourself having a much better experience in your life as an empath.

Chapter 3: Real Life Situations

As an empath, you are bound to go through life just like every other human being on this planet. With that being said, the way that you experience life is going to be entirely different from people who do not have empathic experiences as you do. For that reason, you may feel as the "odd one out" for having experiences that are completely different from what the average person experiences. In fact, it may feel as if you truly cannot talk to anyone and receive any form of compassionate or empathetic advice from people because you are constantly trying to share with people who just do not get what you experience. Understanding how your life experiences are different and how they contribute to you experiencing different aspects of your life can help you begin to understand how you can navigate life as an empath. Below, we are going to explore nine common life experiences as an empath that you are likely to encounter, what they could feel like and what you can do if you have these experiences.

Working Life Experiences

As an empath, often one of the hardest things to do is going to work. In our society, working is considered mandatory, as you need to earn an income in order to be able to afford things like shelter, food, clothes and other basic necessary things in life. For that reason, you know that you are obligated to have a job and earn an income and you likely feel a lot of pressure trying to keep up with this particular aspect of "normal life".

Work can be challenging for empaths for many reasons. The simple fact that it is mandatory and that it requires so much of your time can feel draining and exhausting. On top of that, many empaths find themselves working in environments with toxic bosses and coworkers or with various other factors that suck their energy dry and leave them feeling exhausted at the end of the day. This exhaustion is far different from the normal tiredness that most people feel at the end of the workday. Unlike "normal people", empaths often find themselves completely unable to function due to the stress and exhaustion accumulated from their working life.

The best thing you can do as an empath is to find a way to make your working life more enjoyable. Working for a company that aligns with your values or starting your own company are two great ways to make your working life less exhausting for you. You can also practice having healthier boundaries to remove yourself from workplace drama and avoid being sucked into the energy-draining situations that many workers find themselves in.

Having Hobbies as an Empath

Having hobbies is a healthy and normal way for people to engage in something that is fun and that helps them remain mentally and emotionally healthy. Hobbies have many massive benefits that help us experience better health while also gaining a deeper sense of satisfaction out of life itself. For the average person, hobbies are an easy way to enjoy some of their own time, while experiencing something that brings them happiness.

For empaths, the topic of hobbies can be overwhelming. First and foremost, hobbies are often set aside as the first thing to be ignored when an empath is feeling energetically drained. Because of the way society is structured, this means that many empaths are not even engaging in hobbies in the first place because they truly do not have the energy to devote to it, even if those hobbies would technically help them feel better from being so exhausted.

Aside from the sheer exhaustion, overwhelm and neglect, empaths may also find themselves struggling to engage in hobbies because hobbies can feel like a lot of pressure. Hobbies that involve a group setting or even in a public venue, for example, can expose an empath to a lot of energy, which means that if they are already feeling low on energy, they may not be able to muster up the energy to go. If the hobby requires the empath to be alone, they are more likely to engage; however, if they do not have strong boundaries, they may find this quiet time causing them to feel overwhelmed with memories of an energy drain. To a normal person, this may sound crazy, but to an empath this makes perfect sense. This is how they process all the overwhelming energy that they have been experiencing so far.

If you are an empath and you're looking to engage in hobbies it may be ideal to find a range of hobbies that have varying energetic requirements. This way, you can engage in the ones that feel like a better fit for where you are on a day-to-day basis. You should also have healthy releasing methods so that when you engage in hobbies, you are able to be present in the moment. In addition, you get to enjoy the experience, rather than finding yourself getting overwhelmed with energetic memories and energetic processing.

Handling Wealth Creation as an Empath

As an empath, the current capitalist structure is often overwhelming. The idea of people being paid incredibly low wages to complete tasks that result in certain people getting rich while everyone else suffers seems incredibly painful. For most types of empaths, this is painful, but realizing that they are contributing to this structure when they work at a normal job can feel extremely overwhelming and exhausting to an empath. This alone can make their working life more exhausting, but it can also create a deep conflict around the process of wealth creation. On one hand, an empath knows that they need to create wealth in order to sustain their life and, on the other, they feel guilty if they suspect that the wealth they are creating is being made in any way that harms the environment or other people.

If you find yourself feeling guilty or feeling "dirty" about the money you are earning, there are a few things you can do to begin earning money in a way that feels better for you. Primarily, you can focus on working with a company that aligns with your values and that is genuinely doing good things for the world around you. Being able to work with a company that is contributing in positive ways to the world can make your work feel more meaningful and it can help you align wealth creation by fulfilling your life's mission.

Another way you can work on making wealth creation more peaceful and less conflicting is to consider starting your own business. Many empaths learn strong coping methods for their energetic well-being and then they go on to begin their own companies, so they have complete control over wealth creation and management. This way, they can feel confident that the money they earn is doing good things in the world and that it is being earned in an ethical and sustainable way. Often, empaths will also earn *more* this way, which means they can also afford to spend money in a way that supports ethical and sustainable companies. This makes the topic of wealth far more peaceful and less conflicting to an empath.

Turning your passion or skills into a business has never been easier due to the Internet.

Dealing With Your Health as an Empath

For the average person, health is a fairly simple thing to look after unless they have been diagnosed with some form of illness or they have a serious injury. In this case, they will have clear guidelines of what they need to do in order to protect themselves from having any problematic experiences with their health. For empaths, the topic of health is quite different and it can be extremely confusing and overwhelming. This can be amplified if you find that you are a medical empath or if you have medical empath experiences.

As an empath, you are constantly being affected by outside energy, especially if you do not yet have strong coping methods and boundaries in place to protect your energy. As a result, you find yourself constantly being exposed to strange ailments, ranging from weird pains to unusual symptoms that can rarely be explained by a medical doctor. These can lead to increased stress, which may even result in the empath getting diagnosed with something in the long run because the increased stress can lead to various health concerns.

Aside from health itself, taking care of your health can be a challenge too. Empaths are often sensitive to various chemicals and preservatives that are found in many modern food sources, as well as medications, supplements and other things that are meant to support one's health. This can make choosing a healthier lifestyle just as challenging as choosing the "standard" lifestyle.

The best way to make your health easier to handle is to improve your boundaries and energetic protection so that you are less exposed to the energetic disturbances of other people. Then, you also need to focus on finding healthy tools that you can use. Such tools must be able to support you in taking care of your body without the unwanted side effects. Often, eating a local organic non-GMO diet that primarily focuses on clean fuel sources like vegetables, fruits, grains and legumes is ideal. Some empaths may be able to eat animal proteins, whereas others may not be able to eat them at all. You will need to follow what feels right for your body.

In addition to what you choose to eat, you will also need to be particularly intentional about your sleep schedule, as well as your exercise or workout schedule. You should also incorporate elements into your schedule for mental and emotional wellness so that you can take proper care of yourself. You will also want to work together with a doctor and possibly a therapist who can both be considerate of your sensitivities and support you with navigating a healthier life.

Family Life Experiences

Engaging in family experiences as an empath can go in many ways. Some empaths have highly understanding and compassionate families, whereas others have families that are full of energy vampires and narcissists. Some people have a blended family that includes both compassionate and caring people and energy vampires and narcissists.

For empaths, the hardest part of dealing with family is dealing with the unusual belief that we have an obligation to our family in any way. Pressure from within your family to remain having an obligation to your family can be extremely intense and painful for an empath. If you find yourself feeling that obligation to your family, you are going to need to address this, as this can lead to deep pain and confusion in your life.

The best thing you can do as an empath is to have clear boundaries and avoid being around family members who do not respect them. If you are engaging in relationships where people attempt to pressure you to betray your limits, you need to distance yourself from these people. These experiences may be painful, but they are important if you are going to protect yourself from the abuse that lies within your family.

Most modern empaths have largely surrounded themselves with "makeshift family" or family that consists of some biological family members and family that consists of close friends. This is often referred to as their "soul family" and includes people who respect the empath. They then have to go through rather lengthy healing around the pain that can come from having to abandon your family when they have been abusive and inconsiderate towards you and your well-being.

Having Friendships as an Empath

As an empath, having friendships can feel somewhat challenging, as you may frequently feel pressured to show up in ways that do not feel feasible or comfortable for you. It can be easy to find yourself feeling guilty, overwhelmed and disconnected in relationships, especially if you are trying to nurture relationships that are not being held with other empaths. In general, average people do not know how much energy it takes for you to spend time with them, even if you genuinely enjoy the time that you are spending together. Never mind the energy that it takes to be with them, the energy that comes with any of the activities that you choose together, especially if they are in crowded or "noisy" spaces with lots of energy, can be extremely overwhelming.

Learning how to be around people without becoming wildly overwhelmed is an important part of learning how to handle friendships in a healthier way when you are an empath who wants to have friendships. You also need to learn how to assert yourself and have healthy boundaries so that you are not taking on too much when you are hanging out with your friends. It can be easy for your close one to throw everything at you because you make them feel better and this leads to my next point. Learning how to say "no" to people who do not respect you and how to take time for yourself as it is needed without feeling guilty will play a huge role in your ability to have healthier friendships with the people in your life.

Dating as an Empath

As an empath, dating can be just as challenging as friendships, except it can feel even more complex. When you are trying to date someone new, there can be a lot of pressure in the energy of trying to connect closer to that person and trying to be in a relationship with them. You may find yourself putting far more intense energy and expectations on dates than the other person does because you have to maintain such high standards around who and what comes into your energy field. This can make dating challenging and it can put a lot of pressure on you and your date to "be the perfect fit".

An important way to overcome this particular hardship in dating when you are an empath is to take some time to get to know the person before actually committing to a date with them. You also need to take some time to let go of the idea that everyone you date needs to be a long-term partner. Also, consider having dates in a low-key place that feels more comfortable for you so that you can enjoy yourself more and have a better relationship with your partner. Doing this will prove to be extremely helpful in allowing you to actually relax and enjoy your dates, rather than feeling overwhelmed by the energy and pressure of the entire experience.

Lastly, when you do date, make sure that you trust your energy completely. If you get a weird vibe about someone or you feel as if they are not going to be ideal for you to continue seeing them, cut it off early rather than continuing to see them just to be polite. Respecting your energy in this way will help you avoid being trapped in relationships with people who are not an ideal fit for you and it will allow you to start exercising the benefits of being an empath.

Handling Serious Relationships

If you are in a serious relationship as an empath, this can be incredibly challenging too. Many empaths believe that once they get into a long-term relationship, the pressure of relationships will back off and they will be able to enjoy themselves "like a normal person". The truth is that committed relationships can be fairly challenging for empaths too. You might find yourself regularly being pulled around emotionally and energetically by your partner's emotional and energetic experiences, especially if they tend to be disconnected from what these experiences are and how they feel. In addition, simple disputes or other small arguments may feel extremely painful to an empath because they are very close to the person they are arguing with. This means that you may find yourself feeling extra sensitive around your partner, rather than more "normal and relaxed".

The best thing you can do as an empath in a committed relationship is to learn how to honor your own energy and learn how to have healthier engagements with your partner. You can do this by having healthier boundaries, committing to having proper alone time and giving yourself the space to take care of your energies as you need. The more you can learn to operate as an independent person and maintain your authentic expression, even as a part of a partnership, while also allowing your partner to remain responsible for their own energy, the better your relationship will be.

Meeting Narcissists as an Empath

As an empath, you are going to meet a lot of narcissists. Unfortunately, narcissists are drawn to empaths, like a moth to a flame. They can spot your unique energy and the way that you can naturally give and support others and narcissists love to take advantage of that. In a narcissistic relationship, you are likely to find yourself being mentally, emotionally and energetically abused in almost every conceivable way possible.

The best way to protect yourself from a narcissist as an empath is to learn how to have strong, healthy boundaries. It is also critical that you learn how to spot narcissistic energy and narcissistic people and then refuse to have relationships with these people at all costs. Your ego or inner voice may attempt to tell you that you can "help" these people or that you owe them help in one way or another, but the truth is that you owe them nothing. You owe it to yourself to take care of your energy and distance yourself from people who cannot respect you and your energy. Narcissists will never be able to see the truth and they will always bring you into a vortex of abuse and pain, so all you can do is remove them from your life. You have to learn to spot them so that you do not let new narcissists, at any point in the future, into your life.

Chapter 4: Helping Others

As an empath, your number one purpose in life is to help others. Empaths, as a whole, were born to help the Earth usher into a new, more compassionate existence. You are here to awaken people to the truth of their actions, to protect the Earth from harmful practices and to otherwise work as an energetic and possibly literal activist on the mission of saving the planet.

There are many different ways that this can be done and it is important that you understand that it is not up to you to do all of the different practices that are meant to help heal the planet. It may feel as though a large amount of pressure rides on your shoulders, but the truth is that there are hundreds of thousands, if not millions, of other people just like you who are also taking on this very same mission. Through this, you are all working together to create a more positive experience on Earth while also saving her from the destruction of humanity. It takes each of us fully committing to doing our unique part to create the entire web of healing energy that is needed to reverse the damage that is being done to our planet and our society.

Helping others can come in many ways, such as helping younger empaths identify their true nature and being a guide who shows them the way. You can also support and protect them as they discover their sensitivities and learn to awaken to the energy that exists all around them while supporting them in understanding their own unique gifts and expressing them to the world around them. Another way that you can support the Earth is by simply having empathy for others and by having compassion for what they are going through. In many ways, this very act will help people heal and experience a more positive existence in their lives. Often, this can be done in a simple manner, such as by showing empathy and compassion for your friends and family and working with them to teach them about the truth of who you are and how you are. This way, your friends and family can stop calling you "just sensitive" and start respecting your gifts and even taking your advice as you offer it.

You can also show up for humanity by identifying your unique passion or purpose and learning how to turn this into a side business or even a full-time business so that you can devote even more time to helping. Some empaths have a hard time doing this because they feel guilty charging money for their gifts, but the truth is that the more you are compensated for your gifts, the more you are able to empower yourself and serve your purpose. Through this, your acts of service become far more potent and you are able to do even more for the world, which means that you can completely change the face of humanity as we know it, alongside other empaths.

To help you get a stronger feel for how you can help others while also helping yourself, we are going to dig deeper into what you can specifically do, without draining yourself and your own energy.

Helping Younger Empaths

Every day, new empaths are being born and raised in a society that still largely struggles to support empathic people. The way our society is built and structured is not ideal for young empaths, as it continues to expose them to massive amounts of trauma and overwhelming energy that can make growing up for them difficult. If you had a difficult upbringing yourself because of your own sensitivities, then you can understand exactly what children are going through on a day-to-day basis. Sadly, younger empaths who are struggling to find their way on this Earth are still being exposed to the same struggles that many adult empaths once faced.

Learning to become someone that can show the way for younger empaths means that you give younger empaths the opportunity to understand themselves and their own gifts at a much earlier age. You also give these children or younger empaths the opportunity to step into their purpose and begin helping with healing the Earth at a younger age, which means that you are

30

able to have a better impact on healing the world around you. Being a guide is a big role that adult empaths take on as they grow to understand their own unique gifts and use them responsibly.

Being a guide to young empaths does not necessarily mean that you need to go out of your way to "recruit" younger empaths or find them so that you can help them, although you can do that if you feel called to do it. If, however, creating resources and support systems for massive numbers of young empaths does not resonate with you, you can easily help by making yourself available and supporting those who cross your path. Supporting your own children, other younger people in your family or even those in your friend's families if the relationship buds naturally is a great opportunity for you to begin helping younger empaths feel more empowered and seen in their lives. This way, you can also educate them on what their gifts are, how they can protect themselves and what they can do to live better lives overall.

It is important that if you want to take on the role of helping younger empaths, you also take on the role of helping and healing yourself. Attempting to guide younger generations through their own struggles and traumas when you are refusing to face your own can be challenging and can lead to you having a hard time really supporting these younger ones. You may also end up passing on conflicting or incomplete information that may lead to unfavorable results, such as younger empaths massively struggling to actually feel empowered because what you informed them about may have been tainted by your own projections.

While this does not mean that you cannot help if you are still struggling or healing yourself, it does mean that you should be mindful of what you are saying and the information that you are passing on to younger empaths. You always want to do your best to be as objective and supportive as you can while giving them the ability to feel seen while also feeling free to explore their gifts.

Helping younger empaths is an incredibly noble purpose to take on, no matter what capacity you choose to take it on. Knowing that your own experiences and knowledge are going to support youth in having a better experience than you did can be incredibly healing. It also helps the world in general as these younger individuals can step into and embrace their power much quicker, which results in them being able to help heal the planet much quicker too. The faster we can wake people up, support our fellow empaths and place power in the right loving and caring hands, the faster we will be able to save our planet and our species from the damage that the world is inflicting on it, overall making a much happier world to live in.

Having Empathy for Others and Helping Others Heal

Many empaths feel as though they have to do something significant and special with their gift because they feel a deep sense of obligation to others. This deep sense of obligation can make it hard for you to know how to help others and can make the act of helping others feel like a huge burden or pressure on your shoulders. You may begin to feel as if there is nothing you can do to live up to this expectation because it is so big and challenging, which means that you are going to have a harder time actually showing up for other people.

This overwhelming burden-like feeling often arises in empaths who feel that they have to heal the world and that they are the only ones for the job. Often, empaths forget that there are millions of others just like them who are doing the same thing and that they are not alone in their task. There is plenty that can be done from just one person, but just one person is not responsible for doing everything to heal the planet. You are allowed to have boundaries and to pick and choose when and where you are going to show up and how you are going to show up when you do choose to show up.

Learning how to show up with boundaries means that you can be present more fully when you do decide that you will do this for people. Rather than feeling like you are only allowed to show up when other people need you to, you can take the pressure off and just focus on showing up this one time. That way, you can be fully present and that you can offer the gift of compassion and empathy.

Believe it or not, compassion and empathy are two wildly undervalued and underserved energies in our world. Many people find themselves struggling to get access to an individual who has the capacity to genuinely experience compassion and empathy for them, which is precisely why they may be so attracted to you. For many, you may be the first person who has willingly shown up compassionately and with the capacity to truly understand them. You may not be aware of this or you may be fully aware of this and this may further lead to you feeling like you are obligated to be "the one" for them.

With that being said, you still need to continue realizing that there are other empaths out there. You need to trust that if you choose not to talk to a person or support a person in need, they will come across another empath who can help them. At this point, they are ready to receive the support, which is precisely why they have found you and why they will go on to find another person if you are unavailable to help them too.

For the moments that you are available to support them, though, make sure that you are entirely present. Focus on just letting yourself feel into the natural empathy, compassion and care that rises from within you. Know that you do not have to "train yourself" to experience these things because you were born with the unique gift of being able to feel these energies even without knowing how. For you, these come as a second nature and they make logical sense. Let yourself lean into that natural balance and trust that you can have a stronger impact on others if you focus more on being present and holding your energy than you do if you let yourself be overwhelmed by the burden you have placed on yourself.

Creating and Nurturing Relationships in Your Life

In your own life, you have a lot more power than you think. The relationships in your life have been placed there on purpose — either to help you grow, to help you learn more about yourself or to help you feel nurtured and supported. Chances are, you will find that each relationship in your life serves as a "test" of sorts, so you must be able to understand what those relationships are about and how they are currently impacting your life.

If you have relationships in your life that feel as though they are meant to help you grow or learn more about yourself, you may find that these are either positive or negative. In some cases, you may have these friendships with other empaths who teach you about who you are and what is possible for you and who encourage you to grow into your gifts and become stronger with them in general.

In other cases, you might find yourself in negative relationships where the purpose is to learn about your weaknesses and where you may not presently be taking care of yourself with stronger boundaries. In these cases, you should take these relationships as an opportunity to understand how you are allowing others to take advantage of you and harm you. Take the opportunity to understand how you can eliminate that by being more present and available for yourself. As you learn to handle these negative relationships and set boundaries for yourself, you may find that some naturally grow into healthier relationships and they become more enjoyable and safer for you to handle. On the other hand, some may become even more toxic and you may find yourself with the need to eliminate your relationship with that person so that you are no longer being trapped by that relationship and all of its toxic elements. Sometimes, learning to let go and giving yourself space to decline toxic relationships is an important lesson for an empath.

Relationships that are meant to help you feel supported and allow you to feel safe to be yourself, are naturally healthy and positive relationships that you should continue to nurture in your life. These are the ones that are meant to support you with understanding the value of strong relationships and the value of who you are. Typically, nothing needs to be done in these relationships aside from possibly asserting some of your new boundaries more clearly if you find that some of them are not being respected. Often, you will find that in these relationships, the boundaries were not being respected not because the other person is not respectful, but because the other person had no idea they existed. Once you begin to assert your new boundaries, these individuals will often shift their behaviors immediately and celebrate you by choosing to honor yourself in a deeper way.

When it comes to cultivating new relationships in your life, you need to learn how to understand yourself and what you want and need in relationships on a deeper level. This goes for friendships, romantic relationships and even relationships with your family members. You need to give yourself the space to know who you truly are and what you truly want and need so that when it comes to nurturing and growing these relationships with people, you are able to do so in a way that is respectful towards you.

When you know yourself, including your empathic gifts and tendencies and you know your needs in a relationship, it becomes easier for you to attract and befriend people who can respect that. This is because, if they do not, you can easily assert a boundary and move on to finding the next friend who may be a better fit for you. If this seems exhausting, trust that it does not have to be. You can make friends at your own pace and you can always "screen" people with a few text message conversations before meeting them in person so that you can see how they respond to you. If they seem to have compassion and empathy towards your sensitivities or if they are an empath themselves, they may be a great individual for you to begin building a friendship with. If, however, they make it sound as though you are too sensitive or they do not understand or care for your needs, then they might not be the ideal person for you to begin building a friendship with.

Remember that no matter how deep into a relationship you get, you can always assert your boundaries and respectfully end a relationship if it stops aligning with you. With this in mind, it is safe for you to build relationships as they feel good and leave relationships if they stop feeling good. Choosing to have a relationship with someone in any capacity does not mean you are committed to having this level of relationship with them forevermore.

Building a Business Based on Your Gifts

Another great way that you can really help people with your empathic gifts is through building a business that is based on your gifts. Many empaths find that building their own business is a great opportunity for them to begin building a business that serves their needs in a career and wealth capacity while also being able to show up and serve their mission. For many people, this is an opportunity for them to step away from the soul-sucking energies of being trapped in the corporate world while also being able to give themselves to serve in their mission a lot more frequently. This transition can make the entire career and wealth topics feel a lot more enjoyable and can help free up a lot of energy for the empath.

Choosing to build your own business does not mean that you have to commit to becoming a full-time entrepreneur and running your own business around the clock either. Many empaths run something on the side that allows them to serve their purpose while being compensated for it. For many, this simple exchange makes showing up easier and gives them a better opportunity to have the funds and resources to deepen their gifts while also being able to show up and serve others.

Regardless of whether you choose to build a part-time or full-time business as an empath, you are going to need to focus on implementing some important skills so that you can show up without running your cup empty or burning yourself out. Empaths who get started in their own businesses without taking the time to educate themselves on the new energetic skills they will need often find themselves regretting and resenting their businesses because they can make them feel even more cursed. The reality is that with a few strong, energetic mindset tools in place, being in business can be a wonderful thing and can increase your capacity to serve and feel served in your life.

The biggest mindset and energetic aspect you need to pay attention to is the relationship that you keep between your and your business and the relationship that you keep between your and your clients. Many empaths go into business with no strong boundaries around how they are willing to show up or how often they are willing to show up. Having rules for yourself regarding when you will be present and when you will take breaks is important because this way, you can serve yourself and protect your energy while also being available to serve and help others.

Another boundary you need to have is around whom you are willing to serve. As an empath, you may feel obligated to serve everyone, but the truth is that you are not meant to and that trying to serve everyone is going to burn you out —fast. Rather than trying to burn yourself out over clients who are not ready to change or who are trying to absorb your energy without respecting you, place boundaries around you that will separate you from the people you will be interacting with. Make sure that your clients know that they are required to serve you in a way that is respectful of your energy and that they honor the information you are willing to share.

If you intuitively feel that a client is not ready for the information that you have available for them or that you are constantly giving, but they are never implementing, do not be afraid to "break up" with your clients. Make it very clear that they need to show up ready to receive and implement the guidance you share and that you are not willing to serve people who simply want access to your energy but not your wisdom. This way, you do not

37

feel like you are constantly pouring into clients who are not respectful of your time, energy and information.

Lastly, you need to make sure that when you are working towards cultivating a healthier mindset to serve from, you are serving from a mentality that respects your value. Many empaths feel like they are required to offer things for free or to give heavy discounts for people who are unable to afford their services. The truth is that doing this is only going to result in you having a hard time showing up for your client and them being unable to show up for themselves. Businesses need to get paid and if you choose to go into business, you need to be willing to assert boundaries around the payment. Trust that this is actually an act of service in and of itself, however, as it requires your clients to truly step up for themselves, it also has to respect your need to have an equal energetic exchange that affords you the ability to pay your bills and enjoy life with a full cup.

When it comes to what type of business you can run as an empath, the options are limitless. Empaths can run many types of businesses, ranging from creative businesses to healing and coaching businesses that are used to help their clients. You can pour your artwork onto any artistic medium you desire and let the energy serve your clients or you can pour your own knowledge, wisdom and skills into your clients through energy healing, coaching or other forms of direct service-based help. No matter what you choose to do, make sure that you choose the medium that feels best for you and that helps you serve in the way that you really want to serve others.

Chapter 5: Protecting Yourself From Energy Vampires

Energy vampires are an extremely painful reality for empaths. Virtually every empath who walks the Earth deals with energy vampires. Every single empath in existence has had their own unfortunate experiences with energy vampires. Empaths dealing with such people have to learn about how they can respect their energy and how they can protect themselves from these individuals. If you have not already learned about how you can protect yourself from energy vampires, you are going to need to make this a priority in your life. The sooner you can begin protecting yourself, the sooner you can make being an empath feel more like a blessing and less like a curse. For many empaths, energy vampires are the direct cause of feeling that their blessing is a curse because they have often been exposed to one or many for a lengthy period of time.

No matter how long you are exposed to an energy vampire, the experience itself can be incredibly painful. Furthermore, you might find yourself experiencing an inability to remove these individuals from your life to protect yourself, which can make the experience even more painful. The sooner you can learn how to handle these types of relationships and protect yourself from energy vampires, the better you are going to feel. As a result, more and more your gift will really feel like a gift to you.

Why Energy Vampires Cling to You

As an empath, energy vampires cling to you because they know that you have more powerful and empathetic energy than anyone else on Earth. Energy vampires know that you have a heart of gold and that you will do whatever you can to help anyone in any situation, sometimes regardless of how it impacts you. Often, empaths who are not "trained" to handle their gifts will find themselves struggling to assert boundaries and saying "no" to helping people when they encounter people that are not being helped. To an empath, everyone is deserving and everyone can be saved.

What you believe to be true, is true. Technically, everyone has the ability to look into their own traumas, understand why they crave so much energy from others and heal themselves from this behavior. However, most people will not do so because they are not willing to admit that they have a problem and need support. Plus, they have learned to take advantage of people with loving intentions so that they can continue to behave in a toxic manner and get away with it. For them, engaging in a relationship with you is how they keep you available for the pattern of the abuse and damage that they tend to cause in other people's lives.

You may think that if you stick around long enough and continue to unconditionally love and support someone long enough, they will change, but the truth is that the opposite is actually the case. While unconditional love can heal people, this unconditional love has to come from within themselves, not from others. As for you, you need to realize that if you continue to make yourself available for people like this, you are going to find yourself continually being drained and picked on by others as they take advantage of you. In reality, you are not helping them.

As an empath, it can sometimes feel like you are living life with a revolving door of energy vampires coming in and out of the scene. You may feel as though every time you identify one, assert yourself and free yourself from them, you find that another one pops up in their place. This is likely happening for two reasons. One reason is that you are an empath, so, naturally, they can sense that you are the type of person who will typically let them take advantage of you as they engage in these problematic behaviors.

The other reason is that you may be someone who has yet to cultivate healthy boundaries and coping methods as an empath, which means that you are still susceptible to being mistreated by energy vampires. As you learn how to identify these individuals and protect yourself from them, you will find that you are no longer as vulnerable to their abuse because you know how to take care of yourself.

How You Can Start Protecting Your Energy

Learning to protect your energy as an empath means that you need to learn how to set boundaries in obvious and also more subtle manners. Empaths need to have physical, mental, emotional and energetic boundaries if they are going to be able to completely assert themselves towards others and save themselves from the abuses of other people.

On a physical level, you need to assert boundaries that keep a physical distance between you and people who do not respect you and your energies. If you find that there are people in your life who are consistently taking advantage of you, requesting too much from you or not respecting you, you need to assert a boundary and keep them out of your life. You may be able to allow certain people to take a small amount of time in your life, but others may need to be removed completely. You will need to decide what feels right for yourself.

On a mental level, you need to have boundaries within yourself towards what you are willing to allow and what you are not willing to allow. Often, empaths have conflicting thoughts that state things such as "I need to protect myself, but I also need to help this person —just this once". This type of inner conflicts can continually take you off course and keep you trapped in unhealthy relationships with people. Start asserting to yourself that your protection, safety and energy matter and those people who are a drain on you are not people that you need to support. You are not obligated to help everyone, even if you are an empath.

On an emotional level, you need to have boundaries with yourself as well. Often, empaths find themselves struggling to assert themselves because they become emotionally entangled with other people, which is where the sense of "obligation" comes in. Learning how to identify this type of emotional behavioral patterns ensures that you can identify any time you are being emotionally manipulated or roped into unhealthy circumstances so that you can assert yourself and protect yourself.

On a spiritual level, you need to have boundaries between your energy and the energy of others. This means that anytime you notice someone is emotionally draining, you need to assert energetic boundaries that protect you from them. Often, this comes in the form of energetic shielding, where you visualize your energy being completely encompassed by a bubble that keeps your energy separate from anyone else's. For most empaths, this is done on a consistent basis as a way to protect themselves from other people. For some empaths, however, they may only need to focus on this when they are having a particularly challenging experience with another individual.

Spotting Energy Vampires and Respectfully Avoiding Them

As an empath, it can be incredibly helpful for you to learn how to spot energy vampires and learn how to avoid them in your life. The key as an empath is to learn how to respectfully, empathetically and compassionately avoid energy vampires so that you do not begin to feel like you owe them something. When empaths are able to create these healthy boundaries and protect themselves from energy vampires in advance, they can begin to heal the way they put trust in other people and have relationships with other individuals.

Energy vampires, to put simply, are people in your life who do not respect your energy and who constantly act as a drain to be around. Despite how much you may love and care for them, they are overwhelming to deal with and can make you feel bad for choosing to assert yourself if you decide that you need to put your own energy first. Often, these individuals can be covertly abusive, although some may become overtly abusive if you attempt to assert yourself and protect yourself from the amount of energy that they continually demand out of you.

One really clear way to spot an energy vampire is to pay attention to the people that you feel good around and vice versa. Energy vampires have a tendency to make you feel physically weak, mentally drained or emotionally sick anytime you have spent too much time around them. Often, they will make you feel completely and totally drained and it will feel as if you have to put far too much effort into getting back into "functioning shape" again after you are no longer around them. This type of stress can cause problems for many areas of your body and mind and as an empath, these problems can be even more challenging for you to deal with.

Another sign that someone is an energy vampire comes in the form of how they react to you when you attempt to assert yourself or take care of yourself. Regular, healthy people will typically understand if you need to take some time for yourself to live a normal, healthy life. Energy vampires, however, will not. Often, they will grow incredibly frustrated with you to the point where they begin treating you badly and blaming you or even abusing you for trying to take some time away from them. They may try to make you feel as if you are a bad friend or a bad person because you have other obligations or things that you want or need to take care of in your life.

The third really obvious way to spot an energy vampire is in what happens when you are not around. Energy vampires may completely disrespect your boundary of wanting to take some space or have some privacy by messaging you non-stop, calling you and asking you to give them some of your energy, even when you have already admitted that you need space from them. If this begins to happen, you know that you are dealing with an energy

43

vampire who needs to be released from your life so that you can begin to heal and have a healthier life.

It is important that you understand that no one is exempted from being an energy vampire. Family members, friends and even bosses and coworkers can be energy vampires that you are exposed to on a regular basis. If you are not careful, these individuals can cause great harm in your life and can lead you to have an incredibly challenging time navigating a healthy and normal life. If you start noticing any of these warning signs in an existing or new relationship, it is important that you assert yourself and respectfully begin to decline invites to hang out or chat so that you can preserve your energy.

The best way to respectfully decline an energy vampire is to recognize them, calmly assert your boundary and then uphold it. Energy vampires may push for you to get angry or fight with them so that they can take up more of your energy, but this is not necessary. If they do not respect your space, simply mute their number and their social media accounts so that you no longer let them bother you. This way, you can keep upholding the boundary that you have already respectfully asserted.

Turning Negative Energy Into Positive Energy

When you have been exposed to negative energy, such as the energy of an energy vampire, it is important that you learn how to deal with it so that you do not become trapped in the thinking loops that may be running in your mind. Many empaths do not realize that, once they have been exposed to negative energy, it takes a lot more than just removing themselves from a situation to protect themselves and heal from what they have been through. In addition to removing themselves from the situation, empaths also need to recognize the negative energy that they are now carrying and turn it into positive energy so that they are no longer being weighed down.

Carrying negative energy within you can cause a significant amount of stress and pressure on your body. For many people, this can affect their nervous system, cardiovascular system and other parts of their body. According to Dr. Christiane Northrup, energy vampires can put your body at a lot of risk through this heightened levels of stress. These heightened stress levels are also connected to things like autoimmune disorders, heart disease, depression, obesity and more, so holding onto negative energy and being around energy vampires truly is a health risk for you.

Learning to handle the negative energy and turn it into positive energy starts with you identifying what negative energy you are currently carrying. Often, using a brain dump in your journal is the best way to completely spill out everything that you are carrying within you so that you can get it out of you and start processing it. In many cases, just seeing the information on paper and acknowledging it helps you begin to heal from the troubles you are facing in your life.

Once you have completely drained everything out of your brain and transferred it into your journal, you can start intentionally and mindfully looking for ways to heal these things. Mindfully healing can be done by feeling your way through the pain, reframing your experiences or choosing to see things from another perspective. You can also talk to someone, like a therapist, work with your doctor to help handle any health concerns that have stemmed from these negative feelings or work with other trained individuals who can help you. Many empaths find that working alongside nutritionists, wellness coaches and other individuals who are qualified to help them get their system back on track is incredibly helpful in fully recovering from the troubles they are facing.

As you begin to heal from the negative energy you have been carrying, it will naturally start to make room for positive energy to exist in your life. Through this, you will be able to start bringing on more positive energy that will lead to more positive thoughts, emotions and experiences. This positive energy will be natural, sustainable and something that will support you in having a far better experience in life as a human and as an empath, as you learn how to overcome the trauma of energy vampires.

Protecting and Using Your Positive Energy (Rather Than Giving It Away)

After you have started to transmute your negative energy into positive energy, it is important that you start to protect your positive energy so that you do not find yourself simply giving it away to other people. If you start giving your positive energy to other people, you will find yourself wrapped up in another cycle of letting energy vampires take advantage of you as you take on their negative energy.

There are several ways that you can protect yourself and your positive energy, although most of these ways are going to require you to really pay attention to who you are inviting into your life and how you are sharing your energy with them. In most cases, if you can handle relationships properly and have the right boundaries within yourself towards how you are willing to share your energy, you will find yourself experiencing far more positive relationships with other people.

The first thing you need to do to protect your positive energy is to teach yourself to be okay with telling some people that they are no longer allowed to be a part of your life. Also, make sure that you do not feel obligated to let every new person have access to your energy and your time. You are not obligated to let everyone be your friend, even if you think they mean well. If someone does not resonate with you or you feel that they cannot respect your boundaries, you are not required to build a relationship with them, wait for them to change or try to change them.

You also need to make sure that you lower your expectations around energy vampires so that you stop hurting yourself as you wait for these individuals to become more "available" for you. The truth is that most energy vampires will not change and if they do, it is unlikely that they will change for you. Instead of waiting for an energy vampire to change, you should do your best to lower your own expectations so that you stop feeling hurt whenever they are unable to show up for you. This way, you do not find yourself repeatedly being trapped in a cycle of hoping for better and being let down again.

Another way that you can protect your positive energy is by learning to be more calm and neutral around the people who try to drain your energy. This strategy is called "grey rocking" and it essentially works by not giving any time, energy, attention or emotion to the people who are being inconsiderate towards you and your energy. Rather than letting them get the best out of you and showing them that they have the power to shift your energy, show them that they do not have that power. Even if you feel shifted, do not let them onto that fact. Instead, stay as neutral as you possibly can and then deal with your emotions later when they are no longer around. This way, you can reasonably wade through the emotions and energy they have cast on you so that you can heal properly. Also, this will often help you with minimizing the amount of energy they demand so that they lose interest and leave you alone sooner.

Lastly, you need to make sure that you have people in your life that you can honestly communicate with so that you do not feel as though you are facing everything alone. Find a trusted friend or ally whom you can talk to. This person can honestly tell you what they see from the other side. This way, when you are dealing with someone who seems to be acting out with troubling behaviors, you can speak with these trusted individuals and get an honest opinion. This is a great way to take the pressure off yourself for having to try to figure out what is going on alone while also being able to honestly hear about someone else's opinions. Often, a trusted source will let you know if someone is acting crazy or unreasonable and will generally help pump you up so that you can feel empowered to protect yourself against that individual going forward.

Chapter 6: Self Care for Your Mind, Body and Energy

Learning how to recognize, avoid and recover from energy vampires is not the only form of self-care you need to add to your daily routine if you are going to protect yourself as an empath. As an empath, learning how to create a strong self-care routine for all areas of your life is a vital opportunity for you to take care of yourself and prevent yourself from experiencing energetic burnout.

Many empaths do not realize that they require more self-care and attention to their well-being than the average person. For most empaths, simply doing the bare minimum of taking care of themselves is not enough, as it still leaves them with many gaps in their self-care routine. A great example of what it can feel like when you are an empath with a "regular" self-care routine is like a person being on a treadmill chasing after a result that they deeply want. Rather than making any progress, they run faster and faster and never actually get towards what they truly desire in their life.

Learning how to step off the treadmill of self-care and into the action of actually taking care of yourself in a way that truly helps you feel better is important. Through this, you are able to begin feeling your way into a better reality because you are now actually starting to feel better after taking care of yourself. As a result, you are able to show up more for yourself and for the people you care about in your life, which allows you to feel a lot more satisfied with your life in general.

Understand that self-care as an empath comes in many ways, often far beyond the average self-care that most people engage in. Self-care requires empaths to look at their physical, mental, emotional and spiritual well-being and start to choose practices that will allow them to feel fully cared for in all areas of their lives. Once you learn how to fill your cup properly in life, you will find that you feel a lot better *and* that you show up a lot more effectively, which means that people will gain even more from the help that you offer them. Through this, you actually have a far bigger impact, like you always intended, and you do not feel drained or exhausted in achieving that impact.

The Power of Creating Healthy Boundaries

Healthy boundaries are necessary when you are an empath, which is why we have consistently talked about boundaries so often throughout this book. Boundaries truly are something that empaths struggle with, mostly because they have such an easy time talking themselves out of their boundaries and letting people treat them poorly. To an empath, allowing people to behave this way is an opportunity for them to start helping that individual when, in reality, all they are doing is enabling poor behavior. The truth is: people are not going to respect you or receive your help unless they are ready to and if they are not actively willing to respect you and your boundaries now, they are not ready to be in your life. They are not ready for the help you have to offer them and they will not be able to receive anything you attempt to send their way. Instead, you will find yourself constantly making excuses for people and trying to help them and then wondering why no one listens to you.

One of the biggest reasons why empaths may struggle with setting boundaries is because they often see boundaries as being some form of hurtful or harmful thing that they are placing between themselves and another individual. It is important that you understand what a boundary truly is before you set it so that you can begin to set them confidently and without feeling guilty for needing to set them.

You must understand that, at their core, boundaries are not separation, walls, bubbles or anything used to put a divide between you and another individual. They are also not the act of

50

withholding compassion, care, empathy or energy from another person. What boundaries *actually* are, are essentially "rules" for how we are willing to allow ourselves to be treated by ourselves and others in our lives. When we assert our boundaries, what we are really saying is "I do not feel loved, respected or supported when you treat me that way, so I am asking you to stop". After asserting a boundary, you may offer a more respectful and positive solution so that people can begin to treat you better after. At that point, it is up to them to decide if they are going to treat you better or not.

If someone chooses to continue treating you poorly after you have asserted your boundaries or if they continue crossing your limits, then you need to reassert your boundaries with greater strength. This often means that a consequence must be upheld, such as you leaving the vicinity or ending the conversation so that you are no longer being treated badly by the individual who is not respecting you. Once again, they can choose to change the way they treat you or they can choose to continue treating you poorly. If they choose to continue treating you poorly, then you may need to terminate your relationship with that individual.

Understand that at no point are you holding back anything for that individual. All you are doing is setting standards for how you are willing to be treated and expecting them to respect you and uphold those standards. If they choose not to, then, ultimately, they are the ones who have decided to end their relationship with you, even if they attempt to make you feel like you are the one to blame. You are never wrong for expecting to be treated in a respectful and polite way by the people in your life.

Exercises That Support Your Sensitive Energies

There are many types of exercises that you can tap into to help you support your sensitive energies as an empath. Having an arsenal of supportive practices you can use ensures that anytime you feel your energy dropping or feeling particularly low, you can tap into one of these practices to help you start feeling more uplifted and supported. This is an important way for empaths to handle their energy and emotions in a healthy, compassionate way that allows them to truly get all the way back to fill their cup.

As an empath, one of the best things you can learn to do for yourself is to work with energy. The average person may be able to get by having energy work done exclusively by a professional practitioner. However, you are going to need a lot more support than just that. By learning how to engage in energy work for yourself, you give yourself continuous access to the knowledge and tools that you need to recognize imbalanced energies within yourself and balance and heal them as soon as possible.

One of the best ways you can work with energy is through energy shielding. Shielding your energy means that you visualize an energetic shield coming around you and your energy and preventing any unwanted energy from getting in. While living your life with a shield up at all times is not ideal, as it blocks out *everything,* you can use it when you find that you are particularly drained and cannot possibly work with anyone else's energy at that moment.

In addition to visualizing a shield, you can also spend a few minutes each day visualizing your own energy and noticing any areas where the energy may feel flat or imbalanced. Spending a few minutes lovingly nurturing those energies with your awareness and intention can help you replenish that part of yourself and find your way back to feeling good again.

Aside from visualization, you can also learn about crystal healing, reiki, sound healing or other energy healing modalities that you may be able to perform on yourself. While you will still want to go to a trained healer to aid yourself in getting complete healings on a regular basis, knowing how to engage in these healing practices will help you stay balanced for the days in between your healing sessions.

Daily Routines That Support Your Energy

Having daily routines that support your energy is important as an empath. This way, you can feel confident that you are going to have the energetic support that you need to feel your best and take care of yourself. As an empath, the four best things you can engage in on a daily basis include: taking care of your body, taking care of your mind, taking care of your emotions and taking care of your energy.

For your body, engaging in practices like yoga or aerobics and nourishing yourself with healthy foods is a great way to support your energy and take care of yourself. When your body is properly supported and cared for, your physical space is more likely to be a sound foundation and you are less likely to feel overwhelmed by what is going on in the world around you. You should also focus on hydrating yourself through filtered water. Also, make sure that if you ever have any concerns you reach out to a doctor to take care of your physical body right away. Never let your body go untreated if you suspect that you are in need of support for something in your life.

For your mind, you need to work on using practices like visualization and positive thinking to ensure that you are nourishing your mind with healthy thoughts. Also, anytime you find yourself struggling in life, learn how to validate yourself and your experiences while also taking mindful control over the situation so that you can begin to heal yourself. Learning how to validate yourself and gently take control of your own life experience is a powerful way to protect your mental energy.

For your emotions, you want to make sure that you are feeling through them and keeping them free and clear. Holding onto emotions or bottling them up, especially as an empath, is going to result in you feeling overwhelmed. Having a journal can go a long way in releasing emotions and any thoughts that may be attached to those emotions. You can also focus on meditation, which can help you balance your mind and emotions in a healthier manner.

Lastly, your spiritual energies need to be tended to as well. You can do this by meditating, doing yoga, engaging in color therapy, wearing crystals or otherwise engaging in simple day to day energy healing rituals. You can also support your spiritual energy on a daily basis by learning to use spiritual protection tools like visualized shields and visualizing your energy untangling from another person's energy so that you can keep yours clean every day. Doing this on a regular basis will help you experience a much healthier, energetic experience overall.

Rituals That Fuel Your Positive Energy

In addition to filling your cup up and learning how to be mindful of your self-care routine, you should also focus on learning how to incorporate rituals that pump up your positive energy into your day. For empaths who are left without coping methods, it can be challenging to navigate your day to day life. This can lead to a feeling of being constantly drained, negative or feeling pessimistic. Learning how to fuel your own positive energy through positive rituals is a great opportunity for you to continue healing yourself and experiencing a better life as a result.

As an empath, you want to learn how to pump up your own energy without overwhelming yourself. You can do this using strategies like listening to music, engaging in high energy exercises or even listening to a guided meditation session that is meant to boost your energy. Learning how to use these more subtle, yet powerful, tools can help you start having a more positive experience in your life.

It is important to note that as an empath, there are things that you should *avoid* when it comes to boosting your energy too. For example, caffeine and high-intensity exercise practices may be ideal for some people, but for an empath, they can be incredibly overwhelming. Empaths tend to be highly affected by stimulants and stimulating energy to the point where it can become anxiety-producing and overwhelming. Do not put pressure on yourself to boost your energy in "normal" ways that lead to you feeling highly pressured. Instead, find ways that complement your energy and that can truly help you feel better.

Taking Care of Your Body to Boost Your Energy

Taking care of your body is one of the most underrated ways for an empath to take care of their energy field. Your body is the foundation for everything that you experience on Earth and if it is not properly nurtured, you are going to have weird experiences in your energy field. The part of the body that tends to be most active for empaths is the nervous system, as they are constantly being stimulated by different energies, which can occasionally lead to an overactive nervous system. This problem is more likely to occur in empaths who are not taking proper care of themselves and who are not honoring the importance of their physical bodies. This can be especially heightened by your tendency to dissociate if you find that it can become a coping method that you can use to help you manage the uncomfortable energies of being an empath.

As you learn how to heal from the troubling sides of being an empath and you learn how to take care of yourself, you need to learn how to take care of your body too. Learning how to eat properly, sleeping following a healthy sleeping schedule and respecting your body when it wants or needs something from you is incredibly helpful in taking care of yourself and your energy. Most empaths find that they need to gently find themselves a consistent care routine that helps them feel their best and then they need to adhere to that routine as strictly as possible to ensure that they continue feeling good. For some empaths, disruptions to their self-care routine can lead to unwanted symptoms that make their energy difficult to manage.

If you are not yet fully aware of how to take care of your unique body and your unique needs, I encourage you to get a journal and start now. Begin by writing down all areas of your physical self-care needs, such as food, exercise, sleep, hydration and anything else that seems relevant for you. Then, start documenting how you take care of these parts of your life now. You can then begin to intuitively find your way into new routines that help you feel far better, particularly in the areas where you notice your body needs additional support from you. As you continue serving your body in these ways using your mindfulness and intuition, you will likely find that you start healing and feeling a lot better in your life too.

Meditating to Heal and Nurture Your Energy

Meditating is a crucial self-care ritual for any empath, regardless of how good or bad you think you are at meditating. Whether you choose to meditate daily or only as needed, meditating needs to be a practice that you know how to use and that you use accordingly to ensure that you are taking care of yourself and your energy to the best of your ability.

If you choose to meditate on a daily basis, there are countless short meditations you can use that will help you take care of your energy. Everything from grounding your energy to balancing your energy or even recharging yourself so that you have more energy can be done through meditation. If you are not particularly familiar with meditation and how meditation can help you, using guided meditation sessions from iTunes, Google Music, Sound Cloud or YouTube is a great opportunity for you to tap into meditating some more. These meditations will often walk you through a step-by-step experience so that you can begin taking care of your energy as needed.

Daily meditations can be done as part of a ritual, such as in the morning when you wake up or before you go to bed at night. Or you can simply use meditation at any point throughout the day when you feel that you need the added support of meditation practice.

Aside from simple daily meditation, there are plenty of longer meditation sessions that you can do too. Again, all of the aforementioned platforms have great 30-50+ minute meditation sessions that you can follow to help you achieve a certain outcome if you so desire. Or, if you are not interested in following a guided meditation session, you can always turn on some meditation music or simply sit in a quiet space and meditate all on your own. This way, you can get whatever benefit you need out of meditation to keep yourself balanced and comfortable.

The key to meditating is that you realize that it is a personal experience and it is meant to be used by you when you need it. Many people think that meditating needs to be done a certain way in order to be "right" or that you need to follow some form of strict practice in order to benefit from it. The truth is, just as with any other spiritual practice, meditation is highly personal and is all about what you need and what you choose to make of it. If you want to meditate daily and have a strict routine, then you can absolutely do that and benefit from it. If you would rather do a long, deep meditation once a week to balance your energies as you go forward, then do that instead. If you find that you would rather meditate as needed and have no form of rules or routine around how you do it, then do it that way. Typically, you will get the most out of your session when you stop worrying about the rules and start doing what fits best for you.

Chapter 7: Get Over Negative Ways of Thinking

Negative thinking carries a lot of energy with it, much of which can feel overwhelming and damaging for an empath. You might find yourself feeling trapped in negative thought patterns because you are dealing with so much negative energy around you that it seems impossible to get out of those patterns.

Be aware that not all of your thoughts are going to be *your* thoughts, as empaths can often pick up thoughts associated with another person's thoughts or energies. Empaths have a tendency to carry negative thinking patterns that do not belong to them, which can actually contribute to them feeling sick and overwhelmed just by feeling that energy. For many empaths, this negativity feels like a sickness in and of itself and leads to them feeling completely disconnected from their true energy and their ability to truly thrive in life.

When you learn how to identify a negative mindset and where it comes from, as well as how to navigate it, you allow yourself to heal from this unwanted experience and choose to feel positive and healthy instead. As an empath, this is an incredibly important skill to have as it allows you to return to feeling as though you are connected with your truth. Ultimately, this will contribute greatly to your overall happiness.

Understand That a Negative Mindset Is Easy

It is a good idea that you learn to understand that having a negative mindset as an empath is easy. For the average human, a negative mindset is the default setting because we are programmed with what is called "negativity bias". Negativity bias is a human condition that is supposed to protect us and keep us alive because it keeps us skeptical about the things around us, which means we are consistently paying attention to possible threats to our well-being. Of course, we do not have nearly as many threats on our lives as we may have back when we were living in caves and beating rocks together to start fire. So, we do not *have* to lean towards negativity bias anymore.

The thing is that most empaths already know this and tend to want to have a positive mind naturally because this is what feels good for them. However, most empaths are also surrounded by non-empaths who are equipped with negativity bias and who routinely deny that they have any reason to change their thoughts. Rather than admitting that their mindset is a problem, they would rather cling to the negativity and deny their need to grow.

Being associated with people like this can be challenging as an empath because it leaves you vulnerable to people who carry energy that can "infect" you and suck you into a negative frame of mind too. For that reason, you need to understand that slipping into "negativity sickness" can be easy as an empath and you do not need to blame yourself or feel weak or disappointed in yourself for having this happen. Instead, you are better off to recognize how easy this can be, accept that you have fallen into the trap and consciously choose to heal yourself while also choosing to stay aware of what this trap looks like so that you can mindfully avoid it in the future.

Learn How to "Give Thoughts Back"

As an empath, you can "absorb" other people's thoughts and emotions. This means you can also "give them back". This is part of having boundaries with yourself and it is an essential way to heal yourself from experiencing a negative mindset and negative thoughts. When you start "giving thoughts back" what you are really doing is setting the boundary with yourself that declares that you will no longer let other people's bad thoughts ruin your own energy or experiences.

The easiest way to give thoughts back is to start doing it immediately. Anytime you notice that you are "absorbing" someone else's thoughts, take the time to recognize what is happening and intentionally choose to stop absorbing the thought by mentally saying to yourself "I give this thought back; this is not mine". Each time you do this, you teach your mind that you are no longer available to absorb other people's thoughts and that you have no need for other people's thoughts in your life. This way, you are not even taking those thoughts on, to begin with, so you are not likely to find yourself struggling to know what to do with them.

If you do find that you have taken on someone else's thoughts and you are feeling particularly weighed down by them, to the point where they are starting to feel like your own, you need to start creating a safe space for you to heal from those thoughts. This means that you need to make sure that you no longer choose to have those thoughts and that you decide what you are going to think about instead.

A great way to do this is to start keeping a thought journal. This way, anytime you find yourself thinking thoughts that you believe are not yours, you can write down where those thoughts came from and who they originally belong to. After you have tracked your thoughts, you can begin to challenge the thoughts and consider what you really believe instead. Often, we find ourselves especially susceptible to carrying thoughts that are not our own if we have not taken the time to formulate our own opinion on something, so it is easier to adopt someone else's thoughts instead. When you can sit there and consider what you truly believe is the right thought for you at that moment, you can protect yourself from the negative thoughts you have been carrying.

This way, anytime you find yourself habitually having a negative thought, you can instead think about what you truly believe to be true about the said topic. As a result, as *your* truth aligns so much deeper with you, it will be easier for you to reject the negative and unwanted thoughts that are causing unwanted patterns in your life.

Creating a Life Where You Come First

Empaths are known for chronically putting others first, which is part of the reason that they become so overwhelmed and drained. When you are constantly living in a state of feeling overwhelmed, drained and even burnt out, you might find yourself naturally gravitating towards negative thoughts and emotions because you feel too drained to feel optimistic and hopeful about life. After all, it is incredibly hard to feel good when you don't actually *feel* good.

Learning how to break the cycle of putting others first is an important way for you to begin taking care of yourself and your needs so that you can begin feeling better, which will enable you to have more positive thoughts too. This is as much about your health as it is about your mindset.

As an empath, the mindset is often that we need to give up everything that we have in order for other people to have it. There seems to be a lot of people in need in this world and not nearly as many people supporting these people in need. The truth is: there are a lot of people who *will* be in need of help in this world, but who are not quite there yet because they are still experiencing important levels of growth within themselves. The number of people who are actually ready to receive help is directly proportional to the number of people who are able to provide that help. And with that said, they need you to be in your best condition to help them. Otherwise, you are not truly helping them.

Think about it from a different perspective for a moment. If you were to ask for someone's help and you learned that helping you made them feel incredibly crummy, how would you feel? It is likely that you would feel incredibly guilty, embarrassed and possibly even ashamed for having needed their help. You may feel as if you have to pretend that you no longer need help because you have run them dry and now you feel resentful towards yourself for asking for their help. This is one way that someone you help might feel if they were to realize that you had to put yourself out in order to help them, as no one wants to know that their need for help harms another person as a result.

If the person you are helping does not feel guilty but instead believes that you *should* put yourself out in order to help them, then that person is not truly ready to be helped. This is a person who still holds onto a significant amount of selfishness and struggles to see things clearly. They will take advantage of you and they will struggle to implement any of the tools that you have offered them because they are not ready to truly change.

If you want to truly help another person, you need to start by helping yourself and learn how to put yourself first. When you can give from a place of having an abundance of energy and resources to give, then what you give really has an impact and changes the lives of others. Through this, you find yourself experiencing a far greater ability to achieve what you intended to achieve all along and you find yourself healing from all of the energetic drainages from the past.

Balancing Your Own Energy Before Others'

To elaborate on how you can move from negative to positive thinking by putting yourself first, we must dive into how you need to balance your own energy before you can help anyone else. Balancing your own energy means to take care of your body, mind, emotions and spirit before you can help another person.

You have already come to understand why this is important from the perspective of the person that you are helping, but now we need to take a look at it from your own perspective. First things first: you cannot balance someone if you are not balanced yourself, which means you cannot help someone if you cannot help yourself. This is not just because you won't have enough to give, but it is because you will truly have nothing to give since you are not presently living in integrity with what you are trying to help another person through. Furthermore, you trying to help is going to take you further out of integrity, which leaves you in a negative cycle of feeling like you have to help yet not really knowing how to get started.

If you want to begin helping others, you need to start by fully balancing your physical, mental, emotional and spiritual energy in every way possible. You need to trust that you have what it takes to be balanced within yourself first and you need to know how to live with this balance within yourself too. This way, when you use your energy for helping another person you are not throwing yourself further out of whack.

Think of yourself and all your physical, mental, emotional and spiritual energies like a scale. If you were already imbalanced and had one side weighing more than the other and then you tried to add more to your scale, chances are, you would simply go further out of balance. You would find that not enough gets added to the other side to balance you out, or that too much gets added to the already drooping side, which makes it even heavier. No matter how you try to balance it, you are never going to be able to find that sweet spot because inside you are so mixed up that everything keeps getting thrown off course.

Instead of adding more to your plate and becoming even less balanced, you need to take some of it off and clear yourself out to be able to help others. You need to take the contents of your scale off so that you can support people without throwing yourself out of whack, which, in turn, throws their energy out of whack too. This way, you can truly have the impact that you mean to have without feeling incredibly uncomfortable and imbalanced.

Before you begin trying to help anyone else, heal your thoughts, choose a positive frame of mind and begin to heal your own energy. Through that, you will find yourself feeling clear and free enough to be able to take on the task of helping another person balance their energies, too, without throwing yourself out of whack or throwing your own whacky energies into their field.

The Importance of Positive Self-Talk

The way you talk to yourself has a huge impact on your energy and a huge impact on the way that you think and feel. If you want to begin healing yourself, you have to start healing your self-talk too.

Often, the way we talk to ourselves echoes the way that other people have talked to us throughout our lives unless we mindfully take the time to address our self-talk and heal it so that we begin having healthier conversations with ourselves. If you have not yet taken the time to mindfully become aware of what your self-talk is like and where these conversations are stemming from, chances are you are habitually carrying on conversations that you had with someone else as a child. You may be echoing a particularly critical family member, friend, authority figure or any other member of society in your mind over and over through conversations with yourself in a way that is not contributing to your healing or wellness.

Rather than letting your inner conversations be "by default", you need to start letting yourself intentionally build a healthier and more respectful relationship with yourself through your inner thoughts and conversations. The more that you can do this, the more you are going to find yourself creating a powerful and intentional relationship with your inner voice. As a result, you can begin choosing to have inner dialogues that are empowering and that support you with having a healthier mindset.

If you find that your inner dialogue tends to run on autopilot or you are struggling to change your inner dialogue to something more positive, there are a few things you can do to start helping yourself out of this situation. The first thing you can do is keeping a thought journal and start writing down these dialogues word by word so that you can see how unkind they are. This can help motivate you to end these conversations that you have within yourself.

Another thing you can do is surround yourself with people and messages that are more empowering. Follow empowering people on the Internet, have empowering friends in your life and listen to empowering audio tracks like YouTube videos with affirmations and pep talks so that you can begin to hear what it sounds like to think positively within yourself. As you do this, you will find yourself healing drastically from all your negative self-talk. Through that, you will engage in positive self-talk and begin to experience a happier and healthier life.

Chapter 8: Crystals

Crystals are one particularly powerful way that empaths can begin to protect their energy and themselves from the pain of other people in their lives. Crystals can help you ground yourself, protect you from negative energy, support you with having clearer and more intentional relationships with people, heal your heart and help you with many other energy practices in your life. Most empaths who have become aware of their sensitivities choose to wear crystals in the form of jewelry on a regular basis so that they can be intentional with their energy.

The benefit of using crystals to help heal your energy as an empath is that crystals work on their own without you always having to consciously be "at work" with your energy. This way, if you find that you are going about your day-to-day life and you become exposed to unwanted energies, rather than having to consciously put in the work to protect or ground yourself, you can let your crystal help you. As a result, you will only really need to do the work of *keeping* yourself grounded or protected in any instance that may be particularly overwhelming.

How Crystal Healing Works

Crystals emit their energy in a certain frequency that also has the capacity to subtly shift the frequency of the energy fields that surround the crystal. Wearing or carrying crystals with you on a regular basis ensures that your own subtle energy field is "monitored" and balanced by that crystal's energy throughout the day. This energetic exchange happens without you having to intentionally facilitate it over and over again, as the crystal automatically facilitates the balance simply by being present.

Crystal healing can be done by wearing crystal jewelry, although it can also be done by keeping crystal specimens in your home or using them intentionally in healing sessions. Crystals shaped like wands, spheres and palm stones are all used in intentional crystal healing sessions where the individual receiving the healing will often meditate with them, place them on their body or sweep their body with them to cleanse their energy field. Doing this on a regular basis helps you keep your energy protected and cleansed, whereas wearing crystals on a day-to-day basis will help you with in-between maintenance.

If you are not certified as a crystal healer, you can always find a local crystal healer who can perform a session for you. Most cities have healers who are trained to do proper healings, which means that if you feel you need a more intense energy healing, you can book a session and have it done for you. With that being said, this is optional, not strictly necessary for the healing process.

Crystals for Healing Your Energy

There are five types of crystals that empaths should have on hand to help them with healing. These include rose quartz, malachite, lapis lazuli, fluorite and lepidolite.

Rose Quartz

Rose quartz is an incredibly gentle healing stone that works wonders on the heart chakra and the emotional body of sensitive beings. This particular stone has a very gentle energy, which is why it works so wonderfully for empaths. It is a great and gentle healer and a stone that can add unconditional love and support to your energy field if you are feeling particularly drained.

Malachite

Malachite is a rich green-colored stone that is known for releasing stagnant energy in your field so that you have the power to be yourself. If you are healing from negative thoughts or a painful inner dialogue, malachite will help.

Lapis Lazuli

Lapis lazuli will help you dig into your intuitive gifts and awaken them with greater confidence and ease. If you are an intuitive empath and you want to learn how to use your gifts in a healthier manner without being taken advantage of, lapis lazuli is a great stone to use.

Fluorite

Fluorite is known for helping to balance your chakras and support your psychic and intuitive abilities. This stone also has a subtle neutralizing ability to it that enables it to neutralize harmful or negative energies as it balances your energy field.

Lepidolite

Lepidolite is an incredibly gentle healing stone that helps empaths relieve themselves of the anxiety that they can often feel when they are struggling with inner energetic troubles. Working with lepidolite is a wonderful way to calm your energies when you are feeling overwhelmed so that you can begin to feel better within yourself and your own energy field. Carry this particular stone if you are going to be around people whose energy makes you feel overwhelmed.

How Crystal Protection Works

Crystal protection works in the same way that crystal healing works. Protective crystals emit protective energies into your subtle energy body that make it so that unwanted harmful or negative energies cannot penetrate into your space and create discomfort for you in your life. If you are looking to heal yourself from harmful energies, you will want to wear, carry or decorate your space with protective crystals.

Crystals for Protecting Your Energy

The three best protective crystals that an empath can have are black obsidian, smoky quartz and amethyst. All three of these are powerful in protecting your energy field and keeping your subtle energy body safe.

Black Obsidian

Black obsidian is a dark jet black stone that is known for absorbing negative energies from your field before they can reach your body. You can carry, wear or keep this stone nearby when you are dealing with negativity as a way to absorb it out of your energy field and into the stone itself. This stone should regularly be cleansed using sage or by burying it in a pot of dirt to release the negative energies out of it when you are done.

Smoky Quartz

Smoky quartz is known for being particularly helpful for people who find themselves frequently absorbing lower energies as it transmutes the energy for you. This stone does not need to be cleansed or grounded as it quite literally turns negative energy into neutral energy, which means that the stone itself does not carry any negative energy within it at all.

Amethyst

Amethyst is a bright purple stone that is known for protecting the psyche and psychic energies of an individual. As an empath, you are likely a highly intuitive person and deeply connected to your psychic gifts, whether you realize it or not. Having amethyst on hand will ensure that you are keeping your intuitive energy protected at all times.

Conclusion

As an empath, you have come to Earth for a very special reason and you play a strong role in the healing of our planet. With that being said, you cannot play that healing role unless you take the time to understand yourself and your own energies while learning how to balance your healing gifts.

Empaths often find themselves living in cycles where they run their energy dry and keep themselves constantly too drained to be able to really help anyone. This minimizes their impact while maximizing their pain and suffering, which can make an empath feel more as though this state of being is more like a curse than a blessing.

When you learn how to identify your sensitivities and work with them on purpose, you find the opportunity to begin changing the way you show up in the world. Rather than constantly being at the mercy of ill-intentioned energy vampires, you find yourself protecting your own energy and showing up for the people who truly need your help. As a result, you are able to play a big role in helping people have the type of healing results that they really needed.

In order for you to step into your bigger purpose, you are going to need to take the time to teach yourself how to manage and protect your gifts. You need to learn how to understand your own sensitivities, have compassion for yourself and heal yourself so that you can stop feeling so drained all the time. Once you can begin to heal yourself and take care of yourself properly, you will be able to help others in a way that truly has the impact you intended to have all along, without draining yourself.

Trust that no matter what you hear along the way, empaths were never meant to be born into a life of endless suffering. Choose to see all of the suffering you have experienced until now and start taking back control over yourself and your well-being. Through that, you will be able to truly begin to experience the life of joy and healing that you were meant to experience all along.

Made in the USA
Monee, IL
06 September 2020